W9-CSV-960

Matt Abrahams

# Speaking up

without
FREAKING
Out

**25**
Techniques
for
**Confident,
Calm, and
Competent
Presenting**

**Kendall Hunt**
publishing company

Cover photograph © 2010 Shutterstock, Inc.

**Kendall Hunt**
publishing company

www.kendallhunt.com
*Send all inquiries to:*
4050 Westmark Drive
Dubuque, IA  52004-1840

Copyright © 2010 by Matt Abrahams

ISBN 978-0-7575-7979-0

Kendall Hunt Publishing Company has the exclusive
rights to reproduce this work, to prepare derivative
works from this work, to publicly distribute this work,
to publicly perform this work and to publicly display
this work.

All rights reserved. No part of this publication
may be reproduced, stored in a retrieval system,
or transmitted, in any form or by any means, electronic,
mechanical, photocopying, recording, or otherwise,
without the prior written permission of the copyright
owner.

Printed in the United States of America
10  9  8  7  6  5  4  3  2

# *CONTENTS*

# *PREFACE*

If you've ever felt nervous, doubtful, or insecure about giving presentations or speeches, this pocket book is for you. It provides you with easy-to-use techniques for managing presentation anxiety, whether your audience is composed of coworkers, prospective clients, fellow students, or family and friends.

This book was born out of frustration. For decades, psychologists, biologists, and communication researchers have documented and detailed strategies and techniques for addressing speaking anxiety. However, much of this work remains locked away in academic journals. Further, techniques that do escape to a wider audience via public speaking or business communication textbooks are often insufficient. These texts present what I refer to as the "PB & J" approach to speaking anxiety management: "Practice, Breathe, and Just do it." Although these suggestions have some validity, speaking anxiety involves a complicated mix of physiological and psychological factors. Simplistic "PB & J" advice is not likely to help. Worse, it could even increase anxiety if the suggestions are attempted without immediately successful results.

I hope to remedy this lack of actionable information by providing at least 25 tried and tested anxiety management techniques that you can easily use. Most of the techniques detailed here are based on academic research and have been shown to be effective. As you read this book, you will be able to stockpile several techniques that will help you feel more confident about your presentations. Your end goal: speaking up without freaking out!

# *HOW TO USE THIS BOOK*

I applaud you for taking the first steps to becoming a more confident, calm, and competent presenter! This book will equip you with techniques that you can use to manage your speaking anxiety and enhance your comfort.

This book is divided into four chapters: Chapter 1 describes speaking anxiety, its manifestations, and its negative effects. Chapter 2 describes the main theories about why people feel anxious when speaking and, most important, offers you several specific techniques to reduce speaking anxiety, increase your memory, and bolster your confidence. Chapter 3 teaches you how to resist and stop some self-defeating beliefs and behaviors that perpetuate anxiety. Finally, Chapter 4 addresses how to put all this information to work for you. You will be introduced to three people who successfully applied these techniques to become more confident, less fearful presenters.

A glossary is included that will help you with the more technical, scientific terms found in the book (these terms appear in *italics*), along with two appendixes. Appendix A summarizes the anxiety management techniques presented (these techniques appear in **bold** throughout the book). Appendix B gives additional suggestions for those who are not native English speakers.

As you read, you will come across several "**Try this**" activities. I encourage you to complete the activities as you go through the book, while the related ideas are fresh in your mind. Many of the techniques presented here ask you to reflect and then act on the suggestions made. Take your time and determine what works for you. Some of these techniques require practice over an extended period to be effective and for you to be comfortable with them.

Please note: I spend some time initially classifying and clarifying speaking anxiety. Although I think this background knowledge is useful, I support anyone wishing to jump right in and get to the management techniques.

# CHAPTER 1

*Riiiip.* My anxiety level shot through the roof. It happened early one Saturday morning when I was a high school sophomore, competing in my very first speech tournament. Not only were my teammates and coach present to cheer me on, but the girl I was interested in was also there to see me deliver my expository speech on karate. The butterflies in my stomach, the sweat on my brow, and the quiver in my legs made me more than hesitant to begin, but the prodding from my peers gave me enough motivation to begin my presentation.

Little did I know that my pre-speech jitters were nothing compared to what was to come. *Riiiip.* In front of friends, teachers, parents, and a potential girlfriend, I ripped my pants. Not a tiny tear, but a major, gaping crevasse from back belt loop to fly zipper. The front snap kick I performed during the first 10 seconds of my 10-minute speech was supposed to be action packed and engaging. Instead, it was exasperating and embarrassing. My pre-speech nervousness had me so focused on myriad imagined embarrassing outcomes that I forgot to change into my karate pants—the ones designed to allow full leg movements.

Speaking in public, even when a speaker is prepared and practiced, can lead to dramatic and traumatic outcomes. For this reason, year after year for decades, the *Book of Lists* has reported the fear of speaking in public as the most frequent answer to the question "What scares you most?" In fact, people rate speaking anxiety 10 to 20 percent higher than the fear of death, the fear of heights, the fear of spiders, and the fear of fire. As a student of mine once joked: "People would rather stand naked, overlooking a 30-story fall, covered with spiders and snakes, and on fire than give a speech."

Why is fear of speaking always rated so much higher than other fears and phobias? And, more important, how can you learn to manage and reduce this ubiquitous fear?

## SPEAKING ANXIETY 509346

The word "anxiety" comes from the Latin word "angusta," which translates to a narrowing corridor that presses down on one passing through. Thus, anxiety refers to the concern of not making it through something, like a presentation or meeting. The anxiety that originates from speaking in front of others is known as *communication apprehension*. This apprehension is both the real-time anxiety associated with actually speaking *and* the anxiety that comes with just thinking about speaking. Communication researchers list three distinct phases when communication apprehension is likely to strike: (1) anticipation before speaking; (2) confrontation, the first minute or so of presenting; and (3) adaptation, the last minutes of speaking. Most anxious speakers report their anxiety is highest during anticipation and confrontation and declines steadily during adaptation. This pattern of anxiety reduction is referred to as *habituation* and is attributed to the comfort that comes with realizing that you have made it through the first part of your presentation without major problems.

Research in communication apprehension has shown that excessive speaking anxiety produces a downward spiral. Beyond the negatives associated with apprehension, such as embarrassment and inability to focus, this anxiety leads to additional costly outcomes. First, not only does speaking anxiety cause you to present poorer speeches, but if you're highly anxious, you're also likely to write poorer speeches. Second, people who appear nervous are often judged as being deceptive. Many behaviors associated with nervousness— avoiding eye contact, stumbling over words, pacing around, and the like—are also linked to lying or hiding information. This means that speaking anxiety can negatively influence your credibility and your ability to make the impact you want, because people might question your trustworthiness. And, if these problems aren't enough, being nervous reduces your ability to think clearly, to make effective decisions, and to remember.

Anxiety affects mental processing, which often leads to either panicking or choking. *Panicking* occurs when you can't seem to think clearly or maintain focus—you go blank. *Choking* is when you think too much—your thoughts become jumbled and overly self-conscious. This flustered mental processing results in anxious speakers remembering less. They remember fewer of their ideas and fewer details about those ideas. As a result, anxious speakers often struggle to think of the words and ideas that they want to express. They report a disconnect between their desired message and their delivered message.

Finally, being highly anxious about presenting affects your ability to ascertain your speaking effectiveness. Your anxiety not only negatively skews your ability to judge accurately your own performance, but your nervousness tends to make you misinterpret others' feedback as being more negative than it is.

With all these potential costs in mind, reducing speaking anxiety is important to increasing communication confidence and competence.

 **Try this:** To see exactly how nervous public speaking makes you, access and complete the Personal Report of Public Speaking Anxiety scale at http://www.jamescmccroskey.com/measures/prpsa.htm.

# BEING NERVOUS

## What Does Anxiety Feel Like?

Everything you can do to reduce your anxiety will help if you're a nervous speaker. To figure out which anxiety reduction techniques might be best, you first need to better understand communication apprehension and its effects.

What does it mean to be nervous when speaking? What happens to your body physically when you're anxious about speaking in public? Your muscles get tense. You sweat. Your heart rate speeds up. Your blood pressure increases. You find it hard to breathe. Your perception of time warps so that things seem to take much longer than they actually do. You find it hard to execute fine motor skills like using a laser pointer. These physical symptoms of speech anxiety are not good. In fact, prolonged anxiety such as this can lead to long-term health problems.

In reflecting on these physical changes, you can see that your *fear response*, the physiological arousal associated with public speaking, is the same reaction that occurs when anything frightening happens. For example, these physical responses are the same ones you would experience if you were flying and the pilot said over the intercom, "Uh-oh," just before the oxygen masks suddenly came down. In other words, there's no such thing as a distinct public speaking fear. Public speaking, or your anticipation of speaking, is simply activating your innate fight, flight, fright, and freeze response.

Interestingly enough, if I walked up to you and said, "Congratulations, you just won the lottery. Here's $10 million," you'd experience the same physiological changes. Your heart rate would increase, your blood pressure would go up, you might find it hard to breathe, your muscles might get tense, you might feel butterflies in your stomach, and you might sweat. These are the same responses associated with the inborn fear response. You have only one arousal system and one way of experiencing arousal. The difference is that when you find out you won $10 million, you scream, "Yay!" When you are told you have to give a speech, you moan, "Oh, no!"

So, how you identify your arousal plays a role in how you experience the physical manifestations. That is, your labeling of your physiological response plays an important role in how you manage anxiety. Interestingly, researchers have found that anxious individuals tend to be more acutely aware of their bodily sensations and are more likely to interpret increased heart rate and sweating in a negative way.

**Try** **Try this:** When you experience negative physical arousal (e.g., your heart rate increases, you begin to sweat), remind yourself that these reactions are normal and typical. This is called **relabeling**. These sensations do not show anything beyond your body's normal response to something that is displeasing. In other words, avoid giving these natural responses negative significance.

## What Does Anxiety Look Like?

Your audience can't feel your physical reactions to anxiety, but they can observe the behaviors that result. How do you know when a speaker is nervous? Common signs of nervousness when speaking include *disfluencies* (repeating of words, stuttering, using filler words, such as "uh," "you know," and "I mean"), lack of eye contact, fidgety arms and hands, shallow breathing, swaying and pacing, problems with speaking rate (either too fast or too slow), and plumbing reversal—what is usually wet gets dry (e.g., dry mouth) and what is typically dry gets wet (e.g., sweaty palms and brow). You can categorize these anxiety-produced behaviors as either agitated (involving a lot of movement, fast speech, and multiple disfluencies) or rigid (involving stilted, slow speech, and lengthy pauses).

Certainly, you do not engage in these behaviors on purpose. They arise from the increased *cognitive demand* that results from your speech anxiety. You simply do not have the mental resources to cover the *leakage* of these anxiety cues. It's similar to what happens when a poker player with a potentially winning hand indicates nonverbally to the other players that she thinks she is going to win. In the case of speaking, the anxiety associated with speaking might lead you to reveal your nervousness. Thus, techniques that help you to lighten your *cognitive load*, such as **focused practice**, will allow you to reduce your behavioral anxiety cues and will likely lead your audience to see you as less nervous.

Focused practice involves taking one aspect of your presentation—say, the introduction—and delivering it repeatedly until you become highly familiar and comfortable with it (Note: Do not memorize . . . More on the difference between performance and conversation later.). Next, you would move on to another aspect of your presentation, such as transitioning between two specific visual aids. Your repetitive practice leads to what psychologists call *overlearning*. Overlearning lessens your mental load because your practice has caused the material to become more automated. Ultimately, you feel more comfortable because you do not have to spend valuable mental effort thinking about all the particular aspects of your presentation.

**Try this:** To engage in focused practice, "chunk" your presentation into logical units, such as introduction, conclusion, point 1, transitions, etc. In turn, practice each part separately until you feel comfortable and more relaxed with it. Chunking makes your practice and anxiety much more manageable.

## What Scares You the Most about Speaking?

Academics like to create classification systems to help explain phenomena. Scholars have a communication apprehension classification system that distinguishes among four types. The first type is what is called *trait-based communication anxiety*. Trait-based anxiety is better known as shyness or extreme introversion. Because this type of anxiety has a strong genetic component, few people suffer from true trait-based anxiety—roughly only 7 percent of the U.S. population is clinically shy. Yet, you probably know somebody who's really introverted. Clinically shy people can't take public speaking classes or even read books about speaking. They don't have many friends. They cower at social events. They prefer to stay home. Thankfully, both psychological and medical interventions can help those afflicted with clinical shyness to manage better.

For the rest of us, this classification system has three other types of *state-based communication apprehension* that are caused by or correlated with external circumstances.

In situation-based anxiety, the context in which you are speaking (i.e., room location and number of people) causes your anxiety. For example, you might be passionate about recycling, and you might think it is extremely important to recycle. When you talk about recycling with friends at the dinner table or a coffee shop, you're not nervous at all. But when you have to stand in front of many people and give a speech on recycling, you're nervous. In this case, the situation or context in which the communication occurs causes the anxiety.

Next is audience-based anxiety. Who you are speaking to activates this type of anxiety. Audiences vary in many aspects (e.g., status, expertise, attitudinal similarity), and some of these can provoke more anxiety than others. You might not have any trouble speaking to your peers or family members, but speaking to a manager or potential funder might cause you great trepidation. Power and status are believed to be at the root of audience-based anxiety. You are afraid of the consequences your audience might create for you.

The third state-based anxiety is called goal-based anxiety, and it has to do with what you are trying to accomplish. You might be able to talk to your boss about your work progress or even the latest football score without a problem. But when you ask your boss for a raise or time off, you become nervous. It's the goal you're trying to achieve that makes you nervous.

It helps to reflect on the basis of your speaking anxiety (that caused by the situation, your audience, or your goal). Your anxiety might originate in some combination of these state-based anxieties, but one most likely predominates. By determining which one of these types is the source of most of your anxiety, you can begin to develop a targeted, proactive approach to addressing your fear.

**Try this:** Think about a recent public speaking experience in which you felt anxious. Ask yourself what brought about the anxiety? Were you overly concerned with the situation, your audience, or your goal?

# CHAPTER 2

## WHY ARE YOU SO ANXIOUS AND HOW CAN YOU MANAGE IT?

With a better understanding of communication apprehension and how it is manifested, you can address the fundamental question of how to tackle it. Dealing with speech anxiety involves managing two components: (1) your fear of the fear, which is also known as *anxiety sensitivity*, and (2) your fear of presenting. Sometimes, the anxiety over the fear is greater than the actual threat. Clearly, speaking invokes a fear response for many people. Additionally, being afraid or anxious can be frightening. Thus, you need to make sure that any techniques you use not only improve your speaking confidence and competence, but also enhance your ability to manage your reaction to anxiety.

No single all-purpose speaking anxiety management therapy exists. Rather, you can develop several strategies and skills to decrease your apprehension. Research has identified five major theories that explain why we get nervous, and each theory offers multiple therapies or ways of managing that anxiety. The goal is to find at least one strategy or technique that suits you best for managing your fear. Please note that you are unlikely to completely overcome your speaking anxiety. In fact, you probably don't want to overcome your nervousness entirely. **Managed speaking anxiety can be beneficial** in several ways: It helps you to focus on your speaking task, provides you with energy, motivates you to care about your communicative outcomes, and encourages you to prepare. Of course, reaping these benefits requires you to adjust and adapt to your fear.

## Theory 1: Behavioral Theory

According to behavioral theory, you're nervous because you don't have the skills or know the proper way to speak well, so you are afraid. Think of it this way: If you were a novice skier and someone put you at the top of a double black diamond ski slope, you would be scared . . . very scared. But, if over time you took lessons, practiced, and worked on it, you would be more comfortable. In other words, according to behavioral theory, the way to manage your speaking anxiety is to **develop your speaking skills**. Just by reading this text, you've already begun this skills-fortifying journey.

An added benefit of seeking out presentation skills is that you will find others who share your concerns and desire to improve. One clear way to improve your confidence and reduce anxiety is to **collaborate with others** striving toward the same goal. This collaborative approach is one of the main reasons support groups are so helpful.

**Try** **Try this:** Take steps to develop your presentation skills. Read books, attend public speaking classes, join speaking organizations (e.g., Toastmasters), and analyze successful speakers. By actively learning about speaking and developing skills, you will become both more comfortable with and more competent at speaking.

Behavioral theory points to another therapy that I affectionately call the "**fake it until you make it**" approach. Even if you don't know how to speak well, you have an intuitive sense of what makes for a poor speaker. As you learn speaking skills and gain more confidence, you can actively work on reducing negative speaking behaviors. For example, you know that the lack of good eye contact makes you appear nervous and deceptive, so you can learn to fake good eye contact.

How do you fake eye contact? Try looking at that spot between people's eyebrows . . . you know the place, where if you don't shave or pluck you would end up with a "unibrow." Amazingly, your audience believes you are looking directly at them. Similarly, you know that swaying or leaning is a sign of nervousness or excessive casualness. To eliminate this unneeded and distracting movement, face your feet forward directly under your shoulders, bend your knees slightly, and move one foot an inch ahead of the other. From this position, it is very hard to sway or lean.

By covering up or faking your way through your nervousness, you allow for a counterintuitive psychological truism to take effect: Your actions can lead to your feelings. In other words, act in a competent manner, and you will begin to feel competent and reduce your anxiety. Additionally, since your audience does not know you are faking behavior that makes you appear competent and confident, they treat you as if you are naturally competent and confident, which in turn fuels your feelings of competence and confidence. Try it! Fake it until you make it really work.

**Try** **Try this:** Take time to catalog behaviors of competent and confident speakers. Note their use of eye contact and their stance, movement, and gestures. Practice mimicking some of these actions and see how you feel. Over time, as you enact competent speaking behaviors, you will begin to feel more confident and competent.

Finally, behavioral theory suggests that to overcome the initial spike of anxiety when you begin speaking, you should dedicate extra time practicing the delivery of your talk's first 30 seconds. Going from silence to full presenting—also known as *commencing*—can be a tough transition that brings with it extra anxiety. You can **practice smoothly commencing**: Express gratitude for your speaking opportunity, comment on the person introducing you, or talk about the speaking occasion or venue. By having your first words prepared, you can use the time when you are delivering them to scan the room and get acquainted with your surroundings. Much like a football team that has its first few plays scripted, planning out your commencing sentences allows you to calm your nerves and gain your composure.

Sample commencing sentences:

▶ "Thank you for inviting me to present."
▶ "I appreciate the kind words that (name of introducer) shared with you."
▶ "I am really excited to be here at (name the venue/event)."

**Try this:** On a note card, write your commencing sentences. Practice delivering these lines. Further, practice scanning around the room and looking at your audience.

## Theory 2: Learning Theory

Remember Pavlov's famous experiment with his dogs? He trained them to salivate when he rang a bell because they thought they were going to get food. The dogs had learned to associate the stimulus of the bell ringing with the presentation of food. When applied to speaking anxiety, learning theory says that somehow you have learned to associate speaking in front of others as negative, bad, or nerve-wracking. Perhaps you were conditioned to see speaking as anxiety provoking because you had a bad experience when you were younger, you heard that a friend or someone you care about had a bad experience, or you watched something negative happen in the media. In other words, through *conditioning*, some type of modeling caused you to think that speaking in front of others is a bad thing.

According to learning theory, the way to manage speaking anxiety is to extinguish this fear. *Extinguish* means to get rid of the conditioned association or to replace it with something else. The therapeutic management technique based on this theory is called **visualization**. What is meant by *visualization?* If you've ever played a sport, your coach might have told you to visualize, to think about yourself doing whatever that sport requires— maybe kicking the ball into the goal, having the bat hit the ball, making the ball go into the basket. Research from sports psychology shows that the best way athletes can improve their skills is to practice. The second best is to visualize. You can improve your skills, reduce your anxiety, and increase your confidence just by visualizing.

What would an extinguishing visualization be like? Say you're taking a speech class, and you are troubled by your anxiety level in the class. Here's a sample script that you might use to visualize being in that class. Once you have an idea of what this is like, you can tailor the script to work for you and your speaking situation.

Imagine yourself having to give a presentation in your speech class. It is the morning of that presentation. You wake up. You feel refreshed. You had a good night's sleep. You feel good. You get dressed. You put on the clothes that fit right and make you look good. You feel confident. You go to the class. Traffic is smooth and perfect—no delays. You find an amazing parking space right where you want to be. You walk into the classroom. Your fellow students are ready. They're excited to see you. They're awake and engaged. When it's your turn to speak, you get up in front of your class. You're confident; you're sure of yourself. You know you will do a good job. As you're speaking, your audience pays attention. Everyone understands what you're saying. They're focused. At the end, they give you loud applause, and you know that you communicated your ideas clearly. Your audience understood your message. At the end of class, your teacher tells you, "Good job." You feel good about your performance. You know you did your best. (This script is a modified version of the one used in J. Ayers and T. Hopf's research).

Notice that during this visualization you didn't just focus on the speech. As a matter of fact, you didn't focus specifically on what you were saying at all. Sometimes, for nervous people, trying to relax and focus on what they are going to say makes them more nervous; this is called *relaxation-induced anxiety.* That's *not* the goal of visualization. You're trying to make yourself less nervous. What you do is focus holistically on your entire speaking experience, not any one particular element of it, and try to get yourself relaxed and see positive things happening.

An important key to making this work is to do the visualization early, not just before you speak. You need to do it several days in advance, once or twice a day, because you're getting yourself into a pattern. Remember, you're trying to extinguish and unlearn a negative association and replace it with a positive one.

**Try** **Try this:** Identify a speaking opportunity several days from now. Three days before speaking, when you are in a calm and relaxed mood, take yourself through your own modified version of the visualization script. Repeat this over the next two days. Note how you feel during the visualization and afterward. Further, note how your overall anxiety regarding the speaking abates.

## Theory 3: Biological Theory

Biological theory suggests two explanations for why we experience anxiety: (1) You're made nervous by the onslaught of neurotransmitters and hormones that create and exacerbate your anxiety reaction, and (2) you're nervous when speaking in front of others because you have an excessive activation of your fear response.

### Understand Neurotransmitters and Hormones

To begin, a symphony of chemicals, including cortisol and adrenaline, is released throughout your body when a threat, such as public speaking, presents itself. Some of these chemicals initiate actions (e.g., increase heart rate), whereas others inhibit them (e.g., stop digestion). Pharmaceuticals have been around for a number of years that can short circuit or block the action of fear-induced neurotransmitters and hormones. Drugs like beta-blockers, Valium, and certain classes of antidepressants can reduce some of the symptoms of anxiety. Yet these drugs are not without drawbacks; their use carries with it the risk of addiction, inability to concentrate, and reduced blood pressure.

Researchers have recently found that the oxytocin, which promotes bonding between people, can reduce many of the symptoms of social anxiety. Unlike the pharmaceuticals mentioned above, plenty of oxytocin is produced in your body naturally. Every time you hug a friend, shake hands, or kiss your spouse or child, your body releases oxytocin.

 **Try this:** Prior to speaking, spend some time with a person on whom you can rely for social support. Perhaps you can walk to your presentation with this supportive person. Or, shake hands with some of your supportive audience members. These interactions will **release a burst of oxytocin** in your body, which can naturally reduce some of your speaking jitters.

## Address Excessive Activation

The second biological explanation for public speaking anxiety says people have different reactions to anxiety-provoking situations or stimuli. Some people are more sensitive, have a lower threshold, or respond more strongly than others. Think of it this way: You go to a movie with a friend and something scary happens on the screen. Your friend might almost jump out of her seat in fear, while your own response is minimal. You both saw the same thing, but you each reacted very differently. These personal differences exist for speaking anxiety.

The technique that addresses this biological mechanism is **systematic desensitization**, also known as exposure therapy. Systematic desensitization works to change unconscious associations between some aversive stimulus and your anxiety. It works like this: Over time you expose yourself repeatedly to the thing that makes you fearful, with each successive exposure becoming more real or immediate. Eventually, you get to a point where you can do the thing that frightens you— like flying, walking across a high bridge, or giving a speech—without being nervous.

To begin, systematic desensitization has you identify what happens in your body physiologically when you get nervous. What is the first physical sign of anxiety that you experience? A particular muscle group might tense up, you might start to feel queasy, or you might get a headache. Each person has his or her own physiological trigger that fires first when anxiety sets in. Systematic desensitization asks you to become sensitive to your physiological trigger so that when you begin to feel it, you can use relaxation techniques to short circuit or stop the anxiety response.

 **Try this:** Take a minute to quiet your mind and relax your body. Closing your eyes and taking a few deep breaths should help. Once you feel calmer, think of a recent stressful event. Try to identify what happened first to your body when you began to think of the stressor. This response is likely your physiological trigger.

There are numerous relaxation techniques, such as deep breathing, practicing yoga, or chi gong, and the like. A simple, yet effective technique is **sequential muscle relaxation**. This technique has you progressively tense groups of muscles in your body for a few seconds and then slowly release the tension. For example, start with your feet and then progress to your lower legs, upper legs, torso, and arms. By monitoring your breathing—holding your breath on the muscle contraction for two counts and releasing it slowly for two counts as you relax—you can significantly reduce your anxiety. Once you feel that physiological trigger, use your relaxation technique until you get to a point where you're relaxed.

# Try

**Try this:** While sitting or lying down, talk yourself through the sequential muscle relaxation technique. Begin by tensing and relaxing your toes while monitoring your breathing. Work your way through your entire body until you are tensing and relaxing your forehead. When you're done with this exercise, you should feel more relaxed and notice that you're breathing more fully, calmly, and steadily.

Now, you're ready for the systematic desensitization. If you're trying to feel less nervous standing in front of a large audience giving a speech, you don't start by imagining the thing that makes you most nervous. You start small. So, imagine yourself simply writing a speech. You're not even writing; you're just imagining writing the speech. For many people who are anxious about speaking, this is enough to trigger a nervous reaction. You would immediately invoke your relaxation technique and repeat it until you can relax and get to a point where thinking about writing a speech does not trigger much nervousness. This might take an hour, a day, a week, a month, a year—it can take a long time.

Then, you systematically move to the next level that invokes anxiety, such as actually starting to write a speech. When the anxious feelings start, you again invoke your relaxation technique, repeating it until you can write the speech without feeling anxiety. Next, you might stand in front of a mirror and practice delivering the speech. Again, you would alleviate the anxiety via your relaxation practice. After a while, perhaps a long while, you will have short circuited your exaggerated anxiety response and be able to get up in front of an audience and speak.

Systematic desensitization works. It's a powerful and effective technique. However, it takes time. Some professionals, such as therapists and speaking coaches, devote their practices solely to helping people through this exposure process.

**Try**  **Try this:** Identify five increasingly threatening steps in delivering a speech. Begin by relaxing yourself (see the previous "Try this"), and think about the least threatening of the steps you just identified. When you feel your physiological trigger activate, begin your relaxation practice. Repeat this process until you can envision the threat without having your trigger fire. You are now ready to begin again with the next threatening step you identified.

## Theory 4: Cognitive Theory

Cognitive theory has four aspects to it: (1) framing, (2) negative self-talk, (3) repeated negative attributions, and (4) irrational thinking. For each of these aspects, different anxiety management techniques are derived.

### Reframe the Situation

Many people envision speaking as being like acting. When you perform, you have specific lines you need to speak in a certain way at an exact place. What happens when an actor doesn't say his or her lines at the right time or doesn't stand in the right place? It causes problems for the other actors and stagehands and creates confusion for the audience. Thus, in a performance, there is a right way and a wrong way. This performance anxiety is why many actors and actresses get nervous. They know they could do something wrong.

Giving a speech is not performing. Many people think that it is. They think that there's a right way and a wrong way to give a speech, but there isn't. Certainly, there are better ways, but there is no one correct way. Thus, the first cognitive technique involves what cognitive psychologists call *reappraisal*, which in this case means *reframing* the speaking situation as a conversation rather than a performance. It's just a conversation where you do most of the talking. As in any conversation, your audience provides you with immediate and direct responses—albeit nonverbal feedback. Most people who get nervous about giving a speech do not get nervous when having a conversation about the same topic with their friends or family.

Let's say you're giving a speech on why customers should buy your product. You could sit with your friends and talk about why they should purchase from you, and you would not be nervous. However, if you were asked to get up in front of prospective customers and talk about why they should buy your product, you might get nervous. If you **reframe the situation as a conversation**, and not as a performance, you should be less nervous and more comfortable.

But how do you do this? Simply telling yourself, "Okay. I'm going to converse with you," isn't going to have much of an impact on your nervousness. First and foremost, you should *not* memorize your speech. Memorization is predicated on a right way to say something (the way you memorized it). Rather, work on *extemporaneous speaking*, in which you practice speaking aloud from an outline of key points. You might say these points differently each time, but you are still conveying your central arguments. Additionally, when you practice, don't stand up and deliver in front of a mirror or video camera. Practice by sitting at a coffee table or at a coffee shop with friends or family to talk through your speech. Finally, include the word "you" frequently when speaking. "You" provides a direct, verbal connection with your audience and leads to a more conversational tone and approach. Your rehearsal and practice become a conversation.

 **Try this:** After you have collected your thoughts for a specific presentation and organized them in a coherent manner, invite a friend or two to sit with you and talk with them about your ideas. You are not presenting or performing. Rather, you are conversing.

## Combat the Negative Self-Talk

Most people say a lot to themselves. Often, this intrapersonal communication is negative: "You're going to screw up," "Your hair looks awful," "You're going to forget what you're saying." For those who suffer from speaking anxiety, these negative thoughts are both intrusive and pervasive. Beyond being annoying, these negative thoughts result in a *self-fulfilling prophecy*—you expect something is going to happen and it does, because you make it happen. Here's an example of how it works. You're about to give a speech. You say, "This is going to go poorly." What does that do to you? It makes you more stressed. When you're more stressed, are you going to give a better presentation or a worse one? By virtue of your negative self-talk, you ensured a bad presentation.

The technique for reversing this vicious cycle is simply to replace negative comments with **positive affirmations**. Rather than saying, "I'm going to mess this up," you would say, "This is a great opportunity to share my experience with my audience." Note that this affirmation is not that positive. It's not like saying, "This is going to be the best speech ever!" It's just acknowledging the reality that you have a great opportunity to convey your ideas. When you think that you have a great opportunity, that makes you feel good, which, in turn, makes you more relaxed. The more relaxed you are, the more likely you are to give a good presentation. You're using self-fulfilling prophecy to obtain a positive outcome, not a negative one. Before you even prepare a presentation, you should create some positive affirmations that are relevant and meaningful to you. Then, before you speak, you can consciously say one of these affirmations. Affirmations need not be long sayings. Research from choking in sports has found that simple, one-word mantras (e.g., *focus, calm, fun*) can confer the benefits of more lengthy affirmations.

Sample positive affirmations:

▶ People will listen politely to my ideas.
▶ I will convey my excitement about this topic.
▶ I have presented well on this topic before.
▶ Clarity.
▶ Fun.

 **Try this:** Create a positive affirmation that is meaningful to you. You may select one from this section or write your own. Be sure that your affirmation is short, memorable, and reasonable. Rehearse it aloud. You will be empowered by hearing the affirmation. Be sure to say this affirmation before a presentation. Make it the last thing you say to yourself before you begin to speak.

## Distance Yourself from Your Fear

An *attribution* is an explanation for why things happen. If you're anxious about an upcoming presentation, you will often think very negatively about yourself and the whole speaking situation. You might begin to forecast your failure by explaining why you're going to do poorly: "I didn't get a good night's sleep," "I really didn't do enough research," "I didn't have enough detail." You give all these excuses and justifications for why you're going to fail before you even have an opportunity to fail.

And since it's very easy to live up to your lowest expectations, your attributions lead to your failure.

A useful technique to break this cycle of negative attributions comes from **mindfulness**. Among many other things, mindfulness increases cognitive flexibility and capability. It also teaches you how to observe yourself thinking and feeling. This approach can help reduce the need to explain away your potential failure, put things into perspective, and calm your anxiety. When you are feeling negative or nervous about speaking, say to yourself, "This is me feeling nervous about speaking." This kind of assertion takes you out of the nervousness and instead allows you to observe yourself being nervous. Such distancing affords you the opportunity to calm yourself. You can gain a sense of control.

You can do the same thing when you're angry or are experiencing any charged emotion. Say you're feeling nervous, angry, or jealous. Just take a moment and say, "This is me feeling that way." That little space between you and your feelings allows you to ask, "Okay, now what do I do?" This technique enables you to ask yourself helpful questions rather than living in the anxiety, anger, or jealousy.

**Try** **Try this:** Practice distancing yourself from your emotions. Think of a recent emotional event, positive or negative. While you reexperience the emotion, consciously tell yourself, "This is me feeling X emotion." Experience the space this affords you. Notice that you can think about and evaluate your feelings more clearly, and you are less likely to need to justify your behavior.

## Think About It Rationally

*Cognitive modification* techniques address the irrational nature of our speaking fears. If you think for a moment about the worst thing that could happen to you when speaking in public, you will realize that it isn't really that awful. What is absolutely the worst thing that could happen? You might forget your presentation. Other people are going to think you're stupid or unprepared. Maybe people will laugh at you. The first thing to realize is that you have had moments when bad things have happened. Who hasn't done something foolish? Who hasn't been laughed at or forgotten something important? The key is: You survived! You weren't happy about it. You felt bad. You might have had to make some life changes. But you're still here, often better off than before.

Next, think about the likelihood that your worst fear will come true. If you're afraid of forgetting your speech—that you'll be on the spot with nothing to say—what is the likelihood (from 0 to 100 percent) of that happening? A 100-percent certainty means it's absolutely going to happen, and 0 percent means it's not. When you think about your fear in this way, you will realize that it's a bit irrational. The likelihood of your fear coming true is not equal to the enormity of your fear reaction. **Being rational and recognizing your resilience** in the face of negative outcomes represent the final aspect of the cognitive theory of anxiety management.

**Try this:** Take a minute or two to write down all the fears that come to mind when you know you must give a public speech. List as many as you can, regardless of how silly or strange they may seem. (For example, "I'm afraid I'll forget my speech.") Next, write down (1) what is the worst thing that could happen to you personally and to the audience if the specific fear came true and (2) the likelihood (*as a percentage*) of this fear coming true for you in your next speech. (For example, "I'll embarrass myself, and the audience will feel awkward and laugh at me." "There is a 10 percent chance that I will forget my speech.") Reflect on what you have written. Notice that your fears, while real, are often not imminent or even highly likely. And even if they are, the result of their coming true would not be devastating.

## Theory 5: Evolutionary Theory

According to evolutionary theory, you're anxious because you're worried about the consequences of what you're doing. You're preoccupied with getting an A in class, getting the job, closing the deal, or embarrassing yourself. These are all things that could happen in the future, after you've spoken.

A fundamental tenet of evolution is that status is important. Status refers to your position in a social hierarchy. Ten thousand years ago, when human beings were evolving, possessing high status gave an individual access to the fundamental necessities of survival, such as shelter, sexual partners, and food. In other words, possessing higher status increased your likelihood of survival. Conversely, having low status back then decreased access to essential resources and, thus, the likelihood that you would survive.

Since speaking in front of others is fraught with potentially negative future outcomes, evolutionary psychologists suggest that social anxiety (of which public speaking anxiety is a major component) is adaptive for humans. In other words, your evolutionarily ingrained concern for your social status leads you to worry about the consequences of behavior that might risk your status. Speaking in public represents a very salient threat to your status.

How do you undo this innate fear? Before speaking, **focus on the present** and avoid thinking about the consequences of your actions. Having a present-oriented experience, sometimes referred to as a flow experience or rapt attention, means you're so involved in the present that you lose track of time, external stimuli, and your overall self-awareness. You have likely had moments of extreme present orientation in certain situations, like when you play a sport or musical instrument, or when you engage in a deep conversation with a loved one.

Many techniques are available to help you to become more present oriented. Being physical is one technique. I know a professional speaker who deals with his nervousness by doing 100 pushups immediately before he speaks. After this speaker completes his pushups, he jumps up and then steps on the stage to speak. He carries his present orientation with him, along with a little sweat and tingling shoulder muscles. When you're challenging yourself physically, it's hard to think about the future. I know of another professional speaker who plays a handheld video game immediately before presenting. She sets her watch alarm for the time her speech is to begin and then plays a game like Tetris, which is very engaging. She becomes so involved in playing the game—very present oriented—that she is surprised when the alarm goes off. She simply turns off the device and walks on stage to speak.

Listening to music can also help induce a present-oriented perspective. Find a song or a play list that you find engaging and practice becoming absorbed in it. Using humor can also be a fun way to become present oriented. Watch a funny video clip, listen to a comedy routine, or engage in a humorous exchange. Enjoying a good laugh often involves being highly "in the moment."

Tongue twisters offer another way to avoid future thinking before you speak. It is nearly impossible to say a tongue twister accurately and not be fully engaged and present oriented. Not only can doing this make you less anxious about speaking, but it helps you warm up your vocal cords for speaking.

Activities to become present-oriented:
▶ Listen to music you enjoy.
▶ Engage in mildly intense physical activity.
▶ Repeat tongue twisters.
▶ Watch, read, or listen to something funny.

A much more advanced technique for becoming present oriented is used by some politicians who often give the same speech over and over again but still get nervous. A politician will find someone to give her two random words, such as "green" and "bicycle." She will then work these words into her standard presentation in such a way that it doesn't seem strange. She won't get up and say, "Thank you for coming today green bicycles. We're going to . . ." Rather, she will fold these novel, unrelated words into her normal presentation. Think about what this forces her to do. She has to really focus on what she is saying. She has to be incredibly present oriented.

The ability to live in the moment and not worry about future consequences can be enjoyable, and it can be quite practical. Most adults, however, are future oriented. Thus, the trick lies in practicing techniques that enable you to move into a more present-oriented state when the situation requires it.

 **Try this:** Repeat the following tongue twister aloud three times: "I slit a sheet. A sheet I slit. And on that slitted sheet I sit." If you say it wrong, you say a naughty word. When you were saying it, you probably couldn't focus on anything else. You were very present oriented.

# MEMORY AND SPEAKING ANXIETY

An important consideration in any discussion of communication apprehension is the topic of memory. Many people say they are afraid of forgetting what they are going to say or exactly how they want to say something. Memory research has a lot to say about good mental hygiene for speaking.

## Eat, Be Fit, and Sleep Well

The first piece of advice sounds like something a parent might suggest: Eat healthfully, be fit, and sleep well. Unfortunately, healthy eating often goes out the window when a speaking deadline is fast approaching. However, paying attention to your diet can help alleviate your anxiety as well as improve your memory. Here is a bit of consumption advice: Simple sugars and sweets provide a quick energy boost, which is often followed by sluggishness. Complex carbohydrates, nuts, and oils help in memory formation and retention. So, like a long-distance runner, you might find it helpful to carbo load when preparing a presentation. Caffeine facilitates creativity and productivity, but it also invites jitters and flighty memory. It makes sense to go for the triple mocha latte when preparing a speech, but it's not a good idea just immediately before presenting it. Remember: The effects of caffeine linger in the body for a number of hours. Monosaturated fats like olive oil also help memory formation and retention. Although alcohol might be tempting as a relaxation tool, evidence suggests it causes forgetfulness and "loosens the tongue," which might lead to regret.

**Try** **Try this: Create a meal plan** or menu that itemizes the food and drink you will consume before writing, preparing, and presenting your speech. Have this food and drink handy so you won't be tempted to indulge in things that might cause problems for you.

Exercise plays an important role in both memory and anxiety resilience. Exercise physiologists and psychologists have found that people with low body fat and lower than average resting heart rates handle stressful situations better than those who are not as fit. They respond better to both the cognitive and the physiological aspects of stress. Additionally, physical activity increases lung capacity and bolsters mental focus, two very important aspects of speech delivery. Finally, exercise provides an avenue for releasing pent-up anxiety and stress. Try to go for a quick swim, jog, or walk prior to writing or practicing a speech. The calming effect that results comes not just from getting outside and distancing yourself from the stressor, but also from your body's natural endorphins, which are often released when you exercise.

**Try**

**Try this: Create an exercise plan** that gets you outdoors. Before working on your presentation, take 20 minutes to enjoy your exercise plan. Note how much calmer you are, and observe how much sharper you feel mentally after you are done exercising.

With your stomach full, your body fit, and your mind primed to remember, sleep becomes the next important area to examine. Although much remains unknown about sleep, research shows that good-quality, deep sleep is involved in memory formation. Further, sleep helps with creativity and energy. A good night's sleep helps prepare the brain for learning and consolidates newly learned memories so that you can recall them more easily. When you are authoring and preparing a speech, try to **get a full night's sleep** rather than pulling an all-nighter.

**Try**

**Try this:** When authoring and practicing a speech, be sure to go to bed and wake up at your regular times. Avoid altering your sleep-wake schedule. If you find yourself ruminating over your presentation while trying to fall asleep, keep a notebook by your pillow so you can write down your thoughts and release their hold on you.

## Memory and Location

The location where you practice your presentation should be similar to where you will present it. This concept is called *state-dependent learning*. The context in which you learn helps you learn. For example, if you are going to take an exam in a quiet room, you should study in a quiet room. If you are going to give a speech in a large room with big windows where people are quiet and attentive, you should practice giving the speech in a large room with windows. Practicing in the same place where you're presenting—or at least in a similar place—will facilitate your remembering.

**Try** **Try this:** Reflect on the characteristics of the room in which you will be presenting. Better yet, go explore it if you can. When you prepare and practice your presentation, try to do so in a room similar in design, noise level, brightness, and the like.

## Expect the Unexpected

Anxiety research suggests that we **plan for contingencies**, which are alternate  possible outcomes. In other words, be prepared so that if something goes wrong, you're ready and won't get flustered. It's like the fire safety plan you should have at home: If there's a fire, you know where to go to meet up with your loved ones. If your presentation relies on PowerPoint, and the projector doesn't work, what do you do? Do you panic? Or do you invoke your contingency plan and distribute the handouts you brought? What if you blank out during a transition? Do you walk away from the podium?

Or do you simply glance down at your bulleted list of points on your note card. A plan affords you some piece of mind, allowing you to be less nervous.

**Try this:** Identify three to five situations that could cause you difficulty when you present. Think of problems related to your presentation, your materials, or the environment in which you speak. For example, what if the room is too warm or you need an extension cord? With these potential problems in mind, develop an action plan for each one.

Eating properly, exercising, sleeping well, practicing in the same kind of environment in which you will present, and having contingency plans will enable you to increase your confidence, reduce your anxiety, and improve your memory.

# CHAPTER 3

## PROCRASTINATION, PERFECTIONISM, AND POWERPOINT

A discussion of communication apprehension would be incomplete without some mention of three common issues that tend to exacerbate speaking anxiety: procrastination, perfectionism, and PowerPoint.

### Procrastination

Procrastination refers to the conscious choice to put off your work. When this choice of inaction or distraction relates to speech making, it often increases anxiety. Here's a typical anxiety-inducing cycle: Nervous people know that speech writing and presenting make them anxious, so they put off creating their speeches until the last minute. They don't want to experience the nervousness, and it's easier to put off the work or to become distracted than to confront the task and experience the fear. Do you see what that's going to cause for them? At the last possible moment, they will begin to write their speech with only a very short amount of time available. Further, they have created a situation that provides them little time to refine their presentation, let alone practice it. Beyond creating a speech that falls short of its potential, this procrastination invites spikes in anxiety, not to mention feelings of helplessness and unnecessary guilt from knowing they could have (and should have) prepared earlier. Ultimately, procrastination leads to increased nervousness.

In addition to thinking that delay reduces their anxiety, procrastinators may think they gain a face-saving excuse. If they procrastinate and deliver a less-than-stellar speech, they can always tell themselves, "Well, if I had spent more time, it would have gone better." This built-in excuse only reinforces this vicious, nonproductive cycle.

The trick to avoiding procrastination is to **put yourself on a regular schedule**. Identify your presentation delivery date and map backward to determine your major deliverables. Here are some suggested timeframes. Give yourself three to four full days to practice your presentation. This means it needs to be completed almost a full work week before your delivery date. To achieve this practice period, you need to allow yourself at least five days to author the content (I recommend writing an outline only). You may need to add more time if you require research or rely on others for help (e.g., information, review of your content, or creating your accompanying visuals). That means you need at least ten days to two weeks of working time before your delivery date. Mark all dates on your calendar. Manage your time so that you meet your deadlines. If it helps, create incentives for yourself for every milestone achieved. Further, sharing your goal(s) with others can gain you the support you might need to keep going forward. Simply put, the fix for procrastination is planned preparation. Taking control of your presentation preparation in this manner will bring about better presentations, deeper confidence, and less stress.

# Try

**Try this:** Identify three incentives that motivate you. This could be anything from getting a massage to playing a video game to buying yourself flowers. Use these incentives as rewards for accomplishing the itemized presentation milestones you have chosen for yourself.

## Perfectionism

Planning for, preparing for, and desiring success are all incredibly valuable personal assets. These traits often lead to quality presentations with a manageable level of anxiety. Unfortunately, these beneficial traits, when taken to the extreme of perfectionism, can create more speaking anxiety and trouble. Since perfectionists set incredibly high standards for themselves and their work, they become easily discouraged when they fail to meet them. This sense of failure can paralyze perfectionists and make them reluctant to complete speaking assignments. The need to get it right comes with a huge fear of failing. This fear is made worse in speaking situations because perfectionists know that their failure will be witnessed by the audience. Further, perfectionists are distressed by the number of things that can go wrong in the speaking context over which they have little or no control. Wanting everything to be just right makes them worry about everything.

When perfectionism is harnessed appropriately, perfectionists or perfectionistic-leaning speakers possess many beneficial traits and skills. Their ability to plan and methodically achieve a goal is admirable and helpful to speech making. Their intrinsic motivation and willingness to persist creates laser-like focus. However, perfectionists make a fundamentally flawed assumption about speaking. They assume that giving a presentation is about them as speakers, whereas good, effective speaking is actually about the audience. Competent speakers never ask themselves, "What do I need to say?" Instead, they ask, "What does my audience need to hear?" These two questions might sound similar, but they are very different. By focusing on your audience's needs, you remove yourself from the spotlight. You take away the need for you to be right. Your audience's needs are paramount. In taking this **audience-focused perspective**, perfectionists can breathe a sigh of relief because failure is not related solely to them. If failure does occur, it results from the interaction between the audience and the topic. Thus, by removing the perfectionist from the perfectionism, the fear of failure can be reduced and the likelihood that the audience gets what it needs is increased.

 **Try this:** Think about your presentation topic. Ask yourself, "What does my audience need to know about the topic?" and "How can I ensure that they get the information they need?" The answers to these two questions move you away from thinking that there is only one right way to speak.

## PowerPoint

The greatest presentation helper ever developed can also be the biggest roadblock to effective, low-anxiety presentations. When used well, Microsoft's PowerPoint and all the other visual presentation tools facilitate understanding and let audiences absorb information in wonderful ways. Unfortunately, these tools can also enhance anxiety and often lead to poor presentations. Remember, PowerPoint is not the presentation. Your content and delivery are the presentation. PowerPoint is merely a tool. Far too often, speakers think they are writing a speech when they are only drafting PowerPoint slides. These two acts are different. If you were a pastry chef, it would be akin to spending hours icing a cake without regard to the quality of the cake itself. You must break this association. You write, practice, deliver, and are evaluated ultimately on the presentations you deliver, not on the PowerPoint slides you create. Also, not every speech lends itself to PowerPoint. To see this exemplified, search the Internet for Lincoln's "Gettysburg Address" as a PowerPoint. The power and beauty of this famous oration are stripped away completely when forced into the restrictive confines of PowerPoint.

From an anxiety perspective, creating PowerPoint slides gives you the illusion that you are making progress in crafting your speech. In fact, you are simply creating a glorified outline. Although outlines are incredibly valuable, creating slides takes a lot more effort and time. The result is that you spend so much time creating slides with wipes, fades, and embedded videos that you fail to practice your presentation and lose your focus on delivering the message that your audience needs to hear.

It's not that you should avoid PowerPoint and the like. Rather, try to focus on the content of your presentation via an old-fashioned outline and then practice your delivery. Once you have something to say and are saying it well, then you can create some visuals that are appropriate and enhance your presentation. **PowerPoint should not come first.**

# CHAPTER 4

## PUTTING IT ALL TOGETHER

Finding the right technique or blend of techniques that will work for you is more art than science. As you reviewed each of the techniques described in this book, you likely felt that some would be more helpful to you than others. Take this as your starting point. Review the anxiety management techniques and suggestions and note the ones that resonate with you. Once you have a list of techniques, begin to incorporate them into your speech preparation. Many of these techniques require practice and patience, but with perseverance they should help you feel calmer and more confident. Don't be afraid to eliminate one or two techniques if they don't work for you. Experiment by combining techniques or changing the order in which you practice them.

**Try this:** Refer to Appendix A (Anxiety Management Techniques). Identify three to five techniques that you feel would be most useful to you.

# REAL-WORLD EXAMPLES

To demonstrate how to make these techniques your own, I would like to introduce you to Craig, Alicia, and Jayden. Craig is an executive whom I have coached. His fear of speaking in front of audiences is deeply rooted, and it is the one part of his job that he used to dread. Craig had been told that he often comes off as nervous because he fails to connect to his audience. Based on his introspection and my interrogation, Craig concluded that his speaking anxiety is goal based. Because of his organizational role, he is repeatedly in a position of having to ask partners and prospects to do things they likely do not want to do. He used to come to these presentations feeling there was one right way to deliver so that he could achieve his goal and get what he wanted from his audience members.

After reviewing the same techniques that you just read, Craig and I identified four that not only felt good and reasonable to him, but also helped him address the underlying issues of his anxiety. First, Craig prepares and practices presentations as if he is having a <u>conversation</u>. He routinely sits with a few of his direct reports over coffee and talks through his presentations. Second, before speaking, Craig is sure to focus on the positive <u>affirmation</u> we created. Before starting, he says, "I enjoy connecting with each member of my audience." Third,

Craig looks confident by using the "fake it until you make it" eye contact trick of looking at the spaces between his audience members' eyebrows. Fourth, when he begins to feel anxious, Craig relies on the <u>mindfulness</u> technique of distancing himself from his anxious feelings by saying, "This is me feeling nervous." We dubbed his anxiety management techniques *C.A.L.M.* This mnemonic helps Craig remember the four techniques and has the added benefit of reminding him of his goal.

<u>Craig's C.A.L.M. Techniques:</u>

▶ **C**onverse with the audience.
▶ **A**ffirm abilities.
▶ **L**ook confident.
▶ **M**indful focus.

Like Craig, Alicia uses a memory aid to remind her of the five speaking anxiety management techniques that she finds most beneficial. Her mnemonic is *B.R.A.V.E.* Alicia was born in Europe and learned English in adolescence. While at university, she had to deliver a speech in class. She felt the presentation had gone poorly, and to add insult to injury, her professor told her she was the worst presenter in class. Since that day several decades ago, Alicia has experienced extreme situation-based speaking anxiety. As part of a requirement for her new career aspirations, Alicia took one of my public speaking classes. Together, Alicia and I identified her *B.R.A.V.E.* techniques. First, Alicia finds that her anxiety is lessened when she can be <u>present oriented</u>. To aid in focusing on the present, she relies on her avid enjoyment of Sudoku. Just before speaking, she will complete a Sudoku puzzle. Second, Alicia walks through a <u>rationalization</u> process when her fear flares up. She reassures herself that her biggest fear is unlikely to be realized. Third, to reduce her perfectionist tendencies, Alicia makes her approach to authoring her presentation <u>audience centric</u> by starting from the fundamental question "What does my audience need to hear from me?" This audience focus lessens the importance of her need to get it right. Fourth, she practices a <u>visualization</u> of her impending speech twice a day beginning three days before presenting. Fifth, Alicia finds that <u>exercising</u> regularly gives her perspective on her fear and helps her to sleep better at night.

<u>Alicia's B.R.A.V.E. Techniques:</u>

- ▶ **B**e present oriented.
- ▶ **R**ationally confront your speaking fear.
- ▶ **A**ddress what your audience needs to know.
- ▶ **V**isualize a successful presentation experience.
- ▶ **E**xercise.

Unlike Craig and Alicia, Jayden came up with a speaking anxiety management plan that did not require developing new skills. Rather, he needed to stop enacting behaviors that made his anxiety worse. Jayden is an assistant professor who can effortlessly lecture to his students, but he experiences severe anxiety when he must address his peers. His speaking anxiety is specific to the audience to which he presents. Upon analysis, we discovered that Jayden's tendency to procrastinate worsens his anxiety. Typically, Jayden would wait until the last minute to start creating his PowerPoint slides. He could easily have started earlier, but he continually found himself staying up all night prior to his presentation feverishly authoring slides while downing multiple caffeine-filled Red Bulls. By the time he was ready to present, Jayden was jittery, unfocused, and rushed. He would end up reading his wordy slides and not engaging his audience. Together, Jayden and I developed a new presentation writing process for him. To begin, Jayden starts writing his presentation outline—not his PowerPoint slides—a week in advance of his delivery date. Once he has a detailed outline complete, then he begins creating his slides. With his outline done and a few slides created, Jayden begins to practice his presentation at least two days prior to the delivery date. This process is well documented in a formal schedule that he shares with his wife. In fact, they place the schedule on their refrigerator. This public posting helps keep Jayden focused. Jayden makes sure to work on his presentation after he eats a healthy lunch devoid of caffeine. It was not easy for Jayden to cease his bad habits. Now that he has separated presentation writing from PowerPoint slide creation, altered his diet, and publicly committed to his speech development and practice plan, he finds himself less stressed and is delivering better presentations to his colleagues.

Craig, Alicia, and Jayden have made great strides toward managing their anxiety. They feel empowered over their anxiety, and credit this shift to their dedicated work and their use of the anxiety management techniques described in this book. I encourage you to find one or more techniques that can lead you to the kind of success Craig, Alicia, and Jayden enjoy.

# CONCLUSION

Communication apprehension can be debilitating. The fear associated with speaking or anticipating giving a presentation can lead to many negative outcomes. Learning techniques to minimize this anxiety can help you become a more confident and competent communicator.

You now have a deeper understanding of speaking anxiety and over two dozen techniques to help you manage it. As with any learning, you will need to dedicate time to practicing them. Not all of these techniques will work for you, so you must try out the ones you connect with. Do not panic if you don't notice immediate improvement. These techniques take time to refine before they can become part of your repertoire. Regardless of the techniques you choose, simply knowing that you can have a dramatic impact on your speaking anxiety is empowering.

Remember, the focus of your presentation needs to be on your audience—not you. You need to get out of your own way, so that you can feel confident, calm, and competent in speaking up without freaking out!

# APPENDIX A:
# ANXIETY MANAGEMENT TECHNIQUES

| Anxiety Management Technique | What to Do |
| --- | --- |
| Relabel anxious arousal | When you experience negative physical arousal (e.g., your heart rate increases, you begin to sweat), remind yourself that these reactions are normal and typical. They are your body's normal response to something that is displeasing. Avoid giving them greater negative significance. |
| Engage in focused practice | Chunk your presentation into logical units, such as introduction, conclusion, point 1, transitions, etc. Practice each part until you feel comfortable and more relaxed with each chunk. |
| Acknowledge the benefits of managed speaking anxiety | Remind yourself that managed speaking anxiety helps you to focus and to see things clearly, provides you with energy, motivates you to care about your communicative outcomes, and encourages you to prepare. |

*(continued)*

| Anxiety Management Technique | What to Do |
|---|---|
| Develop needed skills | Take steps to develop your presentation skills. Read books; watch and analyze video clips of effective speakers. |
| Collaborate with others | Attend public speaking classes, join speaking organizations (e.g., Toastmasters), or find others wishing to improve. |
| Fake it until you make it | Catalog behaviors of competent and confident speakers. Note their use of eye contact and their stance, movement, and gestures. Mimic some of these actions. Soon you will begin to feel more confident and competent. |
| Practice commencing | Write out and practice your first sentences. These can express gratitude to your audience or acknowledge the person introducing you, the speaking venue, or the opportunity you've been given to speak. While commencing your talk, scan the room so that you can get a handle on your speaking environment. |

*(continued)*

| Anxiety Management Technique | What to Do |
|---|---|
| Visualize | Walk yourself through an ideal speaking experience. Focus holistically on your entire speaking day, culminating in a successful presentation. Try to get yourself relaxed and see positive things happening throughout the day. Avoid getting into the details of what you say. Be sure to begin your visualizations several days before your actual presentation. |
| Precipitate oxytocin flooding | Shake hands with or hug audience members prior to speaking. This physical connection stimulates the release of the neurotransmitter oxytocin, which will produce a calming effect. |
| Use sequential muscle relaxation | Tense and relax your toes while breathing slowly and deeply. Work your way up your entire body until you tense and relax your forehead. When done, you should feel more relaxed with fuller, calmer breathing. |

*(continued)*

| Anxiety Management Technique | What to Do |
|---|---|
| Use systematic desensitization | Identify five increasingly threatening steps in delivering a speech. Begin by relaxing yourself, and think about the least threatening of the steps you just identified. At the first sign of anxiety, start your relaxation practice. Repeat this process until you can envision the threat without having your trigger fire. You are now ready to begin again with the next threatening step you identified. |
| Reframe the speaking situation as a conversation | Invite a friend or two to sit with you, and talk over with them your presentation. You are not presenting or performing, but rather conversing. No longer will you feel the pressure of there being only one right way to present. |
| Create and use positive affirmations | Create a short, memorable, and reasonable positive affirmation. Rehearse it aloud. You will be empowered by hearing the affirmation. Make your affirmation the last thing you say to yourself before you begin to speak. |
| Practice mindfulness | Say "This is me feeling anxiety" when you next feel nervous about speaking. Experience the space this affords you. Notice that you can think about and evaluate your feelings more clearly. |

*(continued)*

| Anxiety Management Technique | What to Do |
|---|---|
| Rationally confront your speaking fear | Identify your biggest fear about presenting. Next, think about the worst thing that could happen to you and your audience if the specific fear came true. Finally, select a likelihood percentage of this fear coming true for you in your next speech. Notice that your fears are not imminent or highly likely. If they were to come true, the result would not be devastating. |
| Maintain a present-oriented focus | Use techniques that create an expanded present moment where you do not think about future consequences. Listen to music, do physical activity, say a tongue twister, play a video game. |
| Create and stick to a meal plan | Create a meal plan or menu that itemizes the food and drink you will consume before writing, preparing, and presenting your speech. Foods containing complex carbohydrates and monosaturated fats are good to eat. Have this food handy so that you won't be tempted to indulge in less wise choices. |

*(continued)*

| Anxiety Management Technique | What to Do |
|---|---|
| Create and stick to an exercise plan | Design an exercise plan that gets you outdoors (e.g., walking, swimming, hiking). Prior to working on your presentation, take 20 minutes to enact your exercise plan. Note how much calmer you are, and observe how much sharper you feel mentally after you are done exercising. |
| Manage your sleep schedule | Go to bed and wake up at your regular times. Avoid altering your sleep-wake schedule. If you find yourself ruminating over your presentation while trying to fall asleep, keep a notebook by your pillow so that you can write down your thoughts and release their hold on you. |
| Practice state-dependent learning | Reflect on the characteristics of the room in which you will be presenting. Better yet, go explore it if you can. When you prepare and practice your presentation, try to do so in a room similar in design, noise level, brightness, and the like. |
| Develop contingency plans | Identify three to five things that could cause you problems when you present. With these potential problems in mind, develop an action plan for each one. |

*(continued)*

| Anxiety Management Technique | What to Do |
|---|---|
| Create a public schedule | Create a public schedule for the development and practicing of your presentation. Identify three incentives that motivate you. Use these incentives as rewards for accomplishing the itemized presentation milestones you have chosen. |
| Focus on your audience | Ask yourself, "What does my audience need to know about the topic?" and "How can I ensure that they get the information they need?" The answers to these two questions move you away from thinking that there is only one right way to speak. |
| Use PowerPoint wisely | Author your content in an outline format before you create slides. |
| Determine the cultural expectations of your audience | List five to seven of the expectations that your audience will have for a competent speaker. Next, develop a plan to practice these skills in your delivery. |
| Begin your presentation speaking slightly more slowly | Craft one or two sentences to begin your talk that acknowledge your audience and/or speaking situation. Practice delivering your opening line(s) at a slower rate than usual. |

# APPENDIX B:
# ANXIETY MANAGEMENT FOR NON-NATIVE ENGLISH SPEAKERS

Having to speak in public can produce enough anxiety, but if you are not a native English speaker, you might find that speaking in front of others is a truly frightening experience. The anxiety management techniques presented in this book are equally valuable to non-native English speakers. However, two other suggestions might help relieve the added anxiety brought on by speaking in a different language. First, it helps to understand the audience's expectations of native English speakers. Second, if you are concerned about having a heavy accent, there are a few things that you can do.

As pointed out in the discussion of the "fake it until you make it" approach, audience members expect nervous speakers to do certain things. They also expect good communicators to do certain things. These expectations are different in different cultures. For example, competent English speakers from the United States (and Canada) make eye contact, they gesture frequently, and they move around the room. A person who is relatively new to the English language, and perhaps to U.S. culture, needs to understand what the audience is expecting from his or her delivery. In other words, you must try to **determine the cultural expectations of your audience**. To do this, you can (1) ask trusted peers, (2) observe competent speakers, and/or (3) try out what you think is appropriate and see how people respond. Regardless of how you determine the expectations that your audience might have, you need to conform to these expectations.

**Try** **Try this:** List five to seven of the expectations that your audience will have for a competent speaker. Next, develop a plan to practice these skills in your delivery. Consider capturing your practice on video to see if you are conforming to these expectations.

Many non-native English speakers have accents. The added worry about whether the audience will be able to understand what is being said weighs heavily on non-native speakers. This added anxiety often leads speakers who have accents to speak very quickly. This almost ensures that the audience will not understand them.

Practicing your pronunciation and finding a program for accent reduction are two options, but an easier technique exists. Audience members are more likely to accept an accented speaker if the speaker simply begins his or her presentation more slowly. Choose an introductory sentence or two that are not vitally important to your presentation and speak more slowly than you usually do. This slower speech rate allows your audience to adapt and adjust to your accent.

**Try this:** Craft one or two sentences to begin your talk that acknowledge your audience and/or speaking situation (e.g., "I am honored to be here to discuss my topic with you."). Practice delivering your opening line(s) at a slower rate than usual. It might be helpful to you to audio or video record these first sentences so that you can hear if you are speaking more slowly.

Being a non-native speaker adds some extra hurdles to managing your speaking anxiety, but with dedicated practice and extra attention, you can reap the rewards of lessened nervousness.

# GLOSSARY

**Anxiety sensitivity** A person's degree of responsiveness to threatening (i.e., fear-inducing) stimuli.

**Attribution** Explanation ascribed to a particular behavior. It can be positive or negative.

**Choking** An anxiety response that leads to too much thinking. A speaker's thoughts become jumbled and he or she becomes overly self-conscious.

**Cognitive demand (cognitive load)** The requirements that a particular task, such as worrying about a speech, place on a person's ability to think and process information.

**Cognitive modification** Similar to reappraisal (see definition below).

**Commencing** The interval between pre-speaking silence and the beginning utterances of a presentation.

**Communication apprehension** Fear associated with either real or anticipated speaking.

**Conditioning** The learned pairing or association of two unrelated stimuli (e.g., public speaking is nerve-wracking).

**Disfluencies** Verbal interruptions in the normal flow of speech, such as repeating of words, stuttering, or using filler words (e.g., "um," "uh," and "ah").

**Extemporaneous speaking** Presenting that is prepared but not memorized. Often, this type of speaking is highly engaging and conversational in tone.

**Extinguish**  To replace or remove a conditioned association.

**Fear response**  The automatic physiological arousal triggered by a threat, such as public speaking. Also known as the fight, flight, fright, or freeze response.

**Habituation**  Reduction in speaking anxiety that follows the first minute of speaking. Attributed to the comfort that comes with making it through the first part of a presentation without major problems.

**Leakage**  The unwanted revealing of one's emotional state via nonverbal cues.

**Overlearning**  Occurs when a particular skill is repeated or practiced so frequently that the skill becomes automated and, thus, requires less mental effort to perform.

**Panicking**  An anxiety response that leads to a lack of clear thinking and an inability to maintain focus.

**Relaxation-induced anxiety**  The extra nervousness some people feel when they try hard to relax after their fear response has been activated.

**Reappraisal (reframing)**  Cognitive switching in the interpretation of a situation or stimulus from one perspective (e.g., presenting as performance) to another (e.g., presenting as a conversation).

**Self-fulfilling prophecy**  A process by which the expectation that a result will happen leads to the occurrence of that result through conscious or unconscious effort in support of the goal.

**State-based communication apprehension**  Anxiety brought on by factors external to the speaker, such as context, audience, or goal.

**State-dependent learning**  The notion that you remember more information more accurately if you recall the information in an environment similar to the environment in which you learned the information.

**Trait-based communication anxiety**  Innate anxiety resulting from genetic predispositions. Synonyms for this type of anxiety are shyness and introversion.

**Visualization**  The process of forming a mental imagine of your actions or performance. This technique is very effective in improving performance and managing performance anxiety.

# BIBLIOGRAPHY

Ayers, J., and Hopf, T. (1993). *Coping with Speech Anxiety.* New York: Ablex Publishing.

Bodie, G. D. (2010). A Racing Heart, Rattling Knees, and Ruminative Thoughts: Defining, Explaining, and Treating Public Speaking Anxiety. *Communication Education, 59,* 70–105.

Csikszentmihalyi, M. (2008). *Flow: The Psychology of Optimal Experience.* New York: Harper Perennial Modern Classics.

Daly, J. A., and McCroskey, J. C. (1984). *Avoiding Communication: Shyness, Reticence, and Communication Apprehension.* Newbury Park, CA: Sage.

Motley, M. T. (1997). *Overcoming Your Fear of Public Speaking: A Proven Method.* Boston: Houghton Mifflin.

Richmond, V. P., and McCroskey, J. C. (1998). *Communication Apprehension, Avoidance, and Effectiveness,* 5th ed. Boston: Allyn and Bacon.

Tolle, Eckhart. (2004). *The Power of Now: A Guide to Spiritual Enlightenment.* Novato, CA: New World Library.

Wehrenberg, M., and Prinz, S. (2007). *The Anxious Brain: The Neurobiological Basis of Anxiety Disorders and How to Effectively Treat Them.* New York: Norton.

Wise, J. (2009). *Extreme Fear: The Science of Your Mind in Danger.* New York: Macmillan.

# ABOUT THE AUTHOR

Matt Abrahams received his undergraduate degree in psychology from Stanford University, his graduate degree in communication studies from the University of California at Davis, and his secondary education teaching credential from San Francisco State University. Matt is considered a passionate, collaborative, and innovative teacher who teaches group, interpersonal, and business communication as well as public speaking at Stanford University, Palo Alto University, and De Anza College. He is especially interested in applying communication knowledge to real-world issues. He has published several research articles on cognitive planning, persuasion, and interpersonal communication. Prior to teaching, Matt held senior leadership positions at several software companies, where he created and ran global training and development organizations. In addition to his teaching and research activities, Matt is co-founder of Bold Echo Communication Solutions, a successful presentation consulting and coaching practice.